Please Do Not Remove Date Due Slip
From Book Pocket

Palm Beach County
Library System

3650 Summit Boulevard
West Palm Beach, FL 33406

DEMCO

BLOODTHIRSTY PLANTS

AN IMAGINATION LIBRARY SERIES

CARNIVOROUS MUSHROOMS
Lassoing Their Prey?

By Victor Gentle

With special thanks to the people at
the Carolina Biological Supply Company,
and to Professor George Barron, University of Guelph, Ontario,
Dr. Bruce Jaffee, University of California at Davis, California,
and Dr. Hans-Börje Jansson, Lund University, Sweden,
for their kind encouragement and help.

Gareth Stevens Publishing
MILWAUKEE

For a free color catalog describing Gareth Stevens' list of high-quality books and multimedia programs, call 1-800-542-2595 (USA) or 1-800-461-9120 (Canada). Gareth Stevens Publishing's Fax: (414) 225-0377. See our catalog, too, on the World Wide Web: http://gsinc.com

Library of Congress Cataloging-in-Publication Data

Gentle, Victor.
  Carnivorous mushrooms: lassoing their prey? / by Victor Gentle.
    p.   cm. — (Bloodthirsty plants)
  Includes bibliographical references (p. 23) and index.
  Summary: Introduces some varieties of fungi that eat eelworms, describing the damage these tiny worms cause to both plants and animals and the different ways that the fungi trap their prey.
    ISBN 0-8368-1656-0 (lib. bdg.)
    1. Predacious fungi–Juvenile literature.   2. Nematode-destroying fungi–Juvenile literature.
  3. Nematoda–Juvenile literature.   [1. Fungi.   2. Nematodes.   3. Carnivorous plants.]   I. Title.
  II. Series: Gentle, Victor.   Bloodthirsty plants.
  QK604.2.P73G45   1996
  589.2'220453–dc20   96-5608

First published in 1996 by
Gareth Stevens Publishing
1555 North RiverCenter Drive, Suite 201
Milwaukee, WI 53212 USA

Text: Victor Gentle
Page layout: Victor Gentle and Karen Knutson
Cover design: Karen Knutson
Photo credits: Cover (main), pp. 9, 11, 21 © George L. Barron/University of Guelph; cover (background) © Stuart Wasserman/Picture Perfect; p. 5 © Visuals Unlimited/E. Webber; p. 7 © Visuals Unlimited/ John D. Cunningham; p. 13 © Bruce A. Jaffee/University of California at Davis; pp. 15, 17 © Carolina Biological Supply Company; p. 19 © Science VU/Visuals Unlimited

Printed in the United States of America

1 2 3 4 5 6 7 8 9 01 00 99 98 97 96

TABLE OF CONTENTS

FUNGUS: FRIEND OR FOE?

A button mushroom is a kind of **fungus**. So are bread mold and yeast. Most fungi live off dead plants, animals, and **dung**, or grow in soil that has plenty of decaying plant matter in it. Unlike green plants, fungi cannot make their own food from sunlight, air, and water.

Many fungi live happily alongside plants. In many cases, both plant and fungus benefit. They help feed each other. But many other fungi attack live plants and animals and cause diseases in them.

Some fungi specialize in trapping and eating eelworms and other **microscopic** animals. They are called **carnivorous** fungi – fungi that eat animals. Not many people know about these special fungi. *You* are about to become one of the few.

Scientists study carnivorous fungi with a **microscope** and other special instruments.

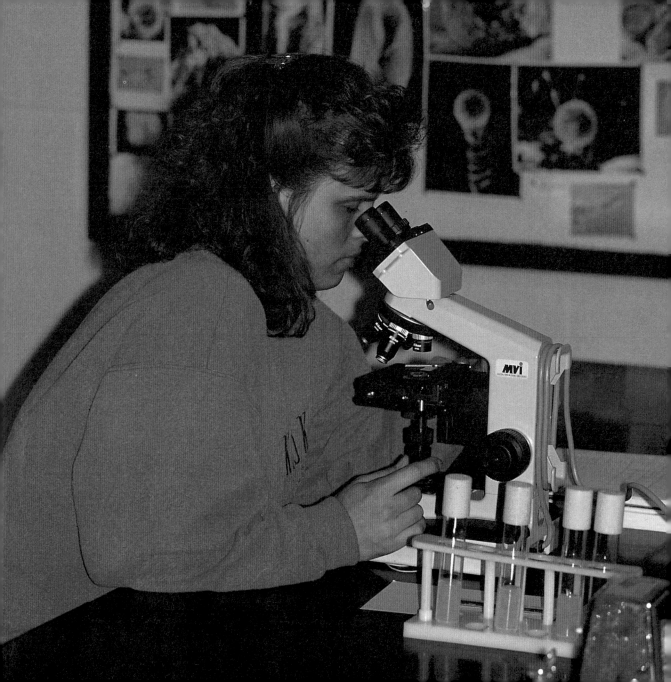

BILLIONS AND BILLIONS OF EELWORMS

We share our planet with trillions of other animals. One of the largest groups is the eelworms – also known as ringworms, nematodes, or helminths. Most of us don't even know they are out there. But in just one square foot of soil (about 1/10 of a square meter), there can be as many as two million eelworms. Imagine, two million tiny, wriggling, simple, wormlike creatures!

Eelworms live all over the world. They live in soils high in the mountains, down deep on the ocean floor, in the Arctic ice cap, and in your backyard.

Many animals and plants have eelworms living inside them as **parasites**. Unfortunately, some of them cause disease, even death.

Most eelworms are tiny, from less than 1/200 to 1/10 inch (0.125 to 2.5 millimeters) long. Others are bigger, a few as long as 25 feet (8 m) or more. These vinegar eelworms are 1/12 inch (2 mm) long.

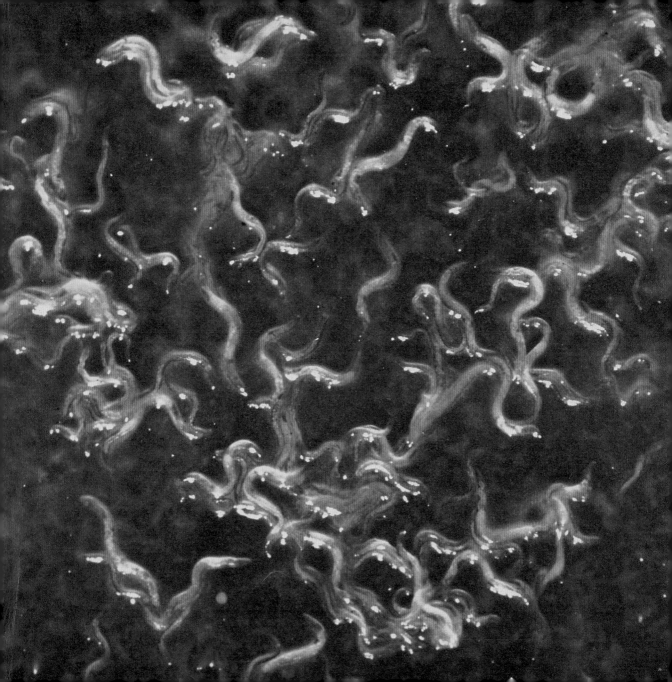

SNAPPING TIGHT, LIKE A LASSO

An eelworm wriggling through soil finds itself attracted toward some curious tiny rings. These rings make a substance that the eelworm finds hard to resist. It decides to wriggle its way through a ring. It presses its body against the inside walls of the ring. Suddenly, in just a tenth of a second, the ring tightens like a lasso! The eelworm is trapped.

The rings belong to a fungus called *Arthrobotrys anchonia* (ar-thruh-BOT-ris an-KOH-nyuh). It has many rings. Each ring is made up of three **cells**. Within a short time after capturing an eelworm, the *Arthrobotrys* starts to grow into it. The fungus devours the eelworm from the inside.

This type of trap is called a **constricting** ring. It is one of six types of traps that carnivorous fungi use.

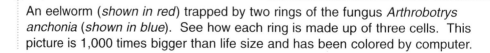

An eelworm (*shown in red*) trapped by two rings of the fungus *Arthrobotrys anchonia* (*shown in blue*). See how each ring is made up of three cells. This picture is 1,000 times bigger than life size and has been colored by computer.

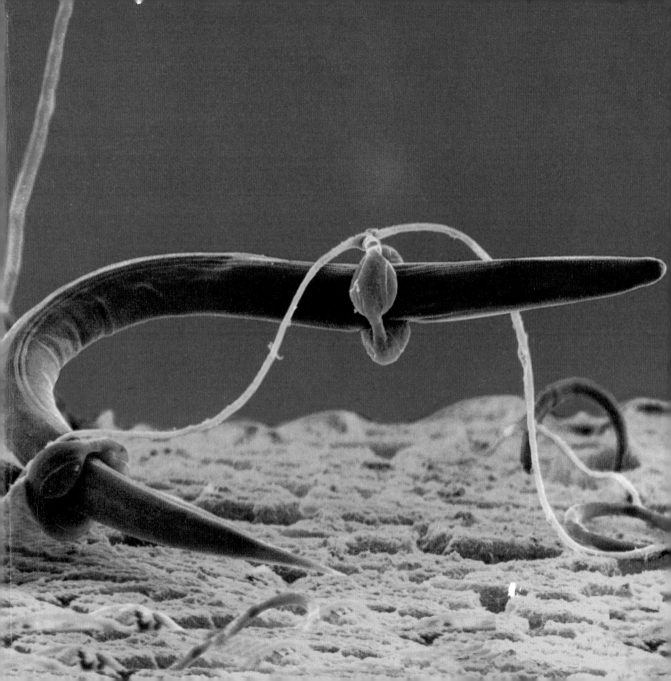

RINGS THAT DON'T TIGHTEN

A fungus called *Dactylaria candida* (DAK-tuh-LAH-ryuh KAN-dih-duh) has rings, too. But these rings don't tighten. Eelworms, often moving quite fast, wedge themselves into the rings. The rings are now just about impossible to shake off.

The eelworms struggle. Often, they manage to break away from the fungus, but with the rings still around them. But it is too late. The rings are alive! Before long, they will pierce the eelworm and grow inside it. The eelworms will die as the new fungi eat them from the inside.

Several fungi have ring traps that don't tighten, just like the rings of *Dactylaria candida*. These ring traps are called non-constricting rings.

The non-constricting rings of *Dactylaria candida*, shown here about 1,200 times bigger than life size.

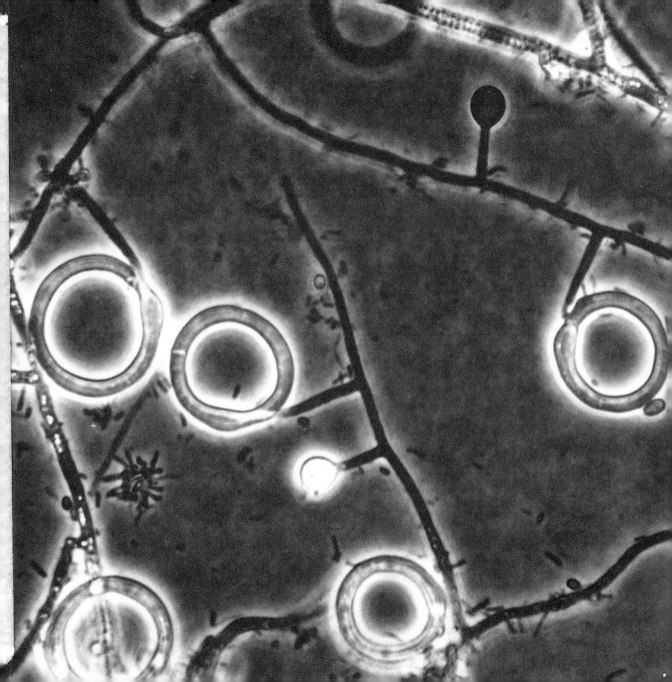

STICKY KNOBS

In addition to rings, *Dactylaria candida* also uses another type of trap — the sticky knob. You can see at least two knobs in the photograph on page 11. Many other carnivorous fungi use sticky knobs as their only type of trap.

At first, scientists thought these knobs were not very good at their job. An eelworm might get stuck for a moment, and then escape. The knobs broke off too easily. It was only later that scientists realized what was really going on.

From the fungus's point of view, it was all right if the knobs broke off. They stayed stuck to the eelworm. Soon, a new fungus would start to grow from the knob. It would quickly pierce the eelworm's skin and grow inside it.

An eelworm is caught on the sticky knobs of the fungus *Monacrosporium ellipsosporum* (muh-NACK-ruh-SPOR-yum uh-LIP-suh-SPOR-um), shown at about 500 times life size.

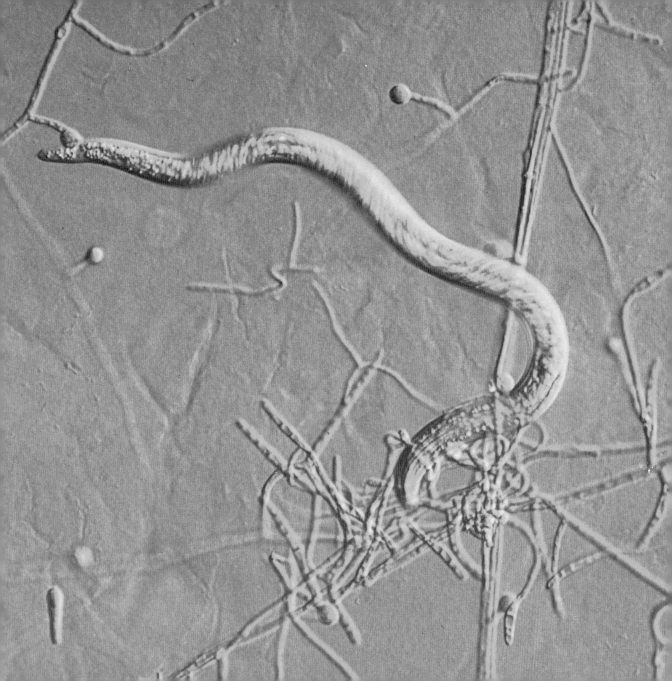

STICKY, STICKY, STICKY

There are three other types of traps that carnivorous fungi use to catch eelworms: sticky nets, sticky branches, and sticky-all-over!

So the complete list of six trap types is:

1. constricting rings
2. non-constricting rings
3. sticky knobs
4. sticky nets
5. sticky branches
6. sticky-all-over

The most common type of trap is the sticky net. These nets can be simple, with just one or two loops. Or they can have many loops joining together in all directions.

The glue made by the nets is very strong. Trapped eelworms hardly ever escape.

Once caught in a net, the eelworm is doomed. Before long, the fungus will start to grow into the eelworm, using it for food. This picture is about 500 times life size.

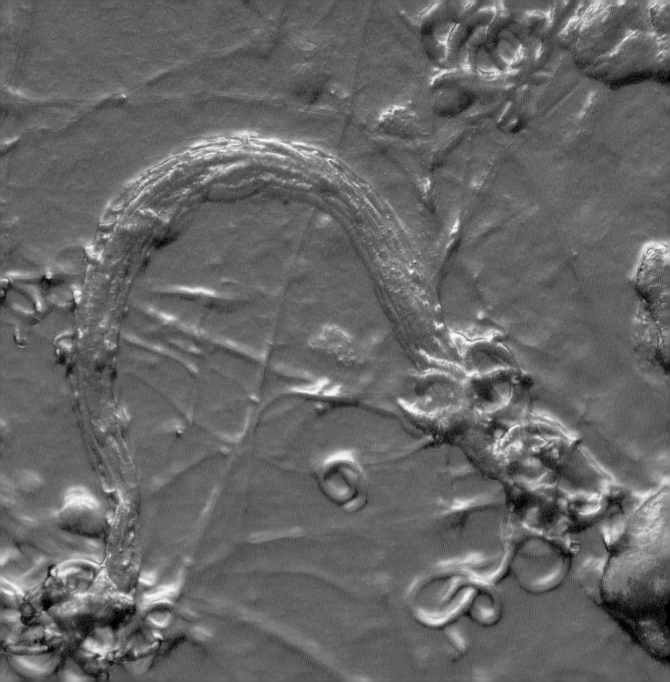

A COW'S BEST FRIEND?

Some eelworms cause diseases in farm animals –
in cows, for example. The pastures where sick cows
graze can become infected, too. This way, eelworms
spread to other cows and young calves.

Recently, scientists in Denmark fed carnivorous
fungi to some young calves. They let the calves
graze in an infected field. The fungus, *Arthrobotrys
flagrans* (FLAY-gruns), protected the calves by
attacking the eelworms. But calves that were
not fed the fungus got sick. The experiment was
a success!

Scientists around the world are studying many
eelworm diseases of cows, sheep, horses, and other
animals. They are learning which carnivorous fungi
are best at fighting which types of eelworms.

A cow grazes peacefully in a field. Sometimes soil
and the plants that cattle eat can become infected
by eelworms that cause disease.

A CARROT'S BEST FRIEND?

Farmers face another big problem with eelworms. Some **species** of eelworms cause root-knot disease. The eelworms attack the roots of crops, causing ugly bumps and weird root growth. As a result, the crops grow poorly or die. Many different crops can suffer from eelworm attack – crops like **maize** (known as corn in some parts of the world), potatoes, tomatoes, and carrots. Some eelworms even eat hot peppers!

It's carnivorous fungi to the rescue again. South African scientists are studying how *Arthrobotrys dactyloides* (DAK-til-OH-uh-deez) can protect maize roots from eelworms. Scientists from South Korea are using another fungus to protect hot pepper roots. In the United States, scientists are working with yet another fungus to beat an eelworm **infection** in potatoes.

18

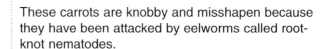

These carrots are knobby and misshapen because they have been attacked by eelworms called root-knot nematodes.

OYSTER MUSHROOMS ON THE PROWL!

Oyster mushrooms, *Pleurotus ostreatus* (pluh-ROE-tus oss-tree-AHT-us), are fancy edible mushrooms that many grocery stores sell. Maybe you have even eaten some yourself.

In 1984, Canadian scientists reported that oyster mushrooms are carnivorous! First, the mushrooms drug their eelworm prey. Then they send out threads that grow into each end of the eelworm and eat it. The scientists were doubly excited. Not only had they found a well-known mushroom to be carnivorous, they had also discovered a new kind of trap — poison droplets!

Every year scientists find new species of fungi that catch and destroy eelworms. No doubt, many more exciting discoveries will come in the years ahead!

These carnivorous oyster mushrooms, safe for people to eat, are being eaten here by slugs. Look closely. But just because you find a slug eating a mushroom *doesn't mean* it's safe for humans. **Never** eat a wild mushroom unless it has been identified by an expert.

THE GREEN WORLD OF CARNIVOROUS PLANTS

Carnivorous fungi have many distant cousins in the green plant world. These green plants are just as fond of an animal snack as our hungry fungi.

There are plants with deadly spring traps, plants with sticky **tentacles,** and plants with tiny, high-speed, vacuum traps. There are plants with greasy curling leaves, and plants with colorful pitfall traps of many shapes and sizes. Find out more about the fascinating world of carnivorous plants by reading other books. And try growing some plants yourself.

WHERE TO GET CARNIVOROUS PLANTS TO STUDY

You can get a carnivorous fungi kit, and many other carnivorous plants and growing containers from:

The Carolina Biological Supply Company
2700 York Road
Burlington, NC 27215

If you are ordering from outside the United States, you may need a special import permit from your government's department of agriculture. Better still, you may be able to find a local supplier. Check telephone directories under "science supplies" or "biological supplies." Or, write to the Carolina Biological Supply Company. They may be able to recommend a supplier for you.

MORE TO READ AND VIEW

Books (nonfiction): *Bladderworts: Trapdoors to Oblivion.* Victor Gentle (Gareth Stevens)
Butterworts: Greasy Cups of Death. Victor Gentle (Gareth Stevens)
Carnivorous Plants. Nancy J. Nielsen (Franklin Watts)
Killer Plants. Mycol Doyle (Lowell House Juvenile)
Pitcher Plants: The Elegant Insect Traps. Carol Lerner (Morrow)
Pitcher Plants: Slippery Pits of No Escape. Victor Gentle (Gareth Stevens)
Plants of Prey. Densey Clyne (Gareth Stevens)
Sundews: A Sweet and Sticky Death. Victor Gentle (Gareth Stevens)
Venus Fly Traps and Waterwheels. Victor Gentle (Gareth Stevens)
Books (fiction): *Elizabite: Adventures of a Carnivorous Plant.* H.A. Rey (Linnet)
Island of Doom. Richard Brightfield (Gareth Stevens)
Videos (nonfiction): *Carnivorous Plants.* (Oxford Scientific Films)
Videos (fiction): *The Day of the Triffids* and *The Little Shop of Horrors* are fun to watch.

WHERE TO WRITE TO FIND OUT MORE

Your community may have a local chapter of a carnivorous plant society. Try looking it up in the telephone directory. Or contact one of the following national organizations:

Australia
Australian Carnivorous Plant Society, Inc.
P.O. Box 391
St. Agnes, South Australia 5097 Australia

New Zealand
New Zealand Carnivorous Plant Society
P.O. Box 21-381, Henderson
Auckland, New Zealand

United Kingdom
The Carnivorous Plant Society
174 Baldwins Lane, Croxley Green
Hertfordshire WD3 3LQ
England

Canada
Eastern Carnivorous Plant Society
Dionaea, 23 Cherryhill Drive
Grimsby, Ontario, Canada L3M 3B3

South Africa – has no CP society, but
a supplier to contact is:
Eric Green, 11 Wepener Street
Southfield, 7800, Cape, South Africa

United States
International Carnivorous Plant Society
Fullerton Arboretum
California State University at Fullerton
Fullerton, CA 92634 USA

If you are on the Internet, or otherwise on-line, you can call up a World Wide Web page that gives links to other Web pages of interest to carnivorous plant enthusiasts: http://www.cvp.com/feedme/links.html

GLOSSARY

You can find these words on the pages listed. Reading a word in a sentence helps you understand it even better.

carnivorous (kar-NIV-er-us) — flesh-eating 4, 8, 12, 14, 16, 18, 20, 22

cells (SELS) — the smallest units, or "building blocks," of plants and animals 8

constricting (kun-STRIK-ting) — tightening 8, 10, 14

dung (DUNG) — solid waste of animals 4

fungus (FUNG-us) — plural: **fungi** — a fungus is a kind of plant whose main feature is that it has none of the special green substance found in most leafy plants, so it can't make its own food from sunlight, air, and water 4, 8, 10, 12, 14, 16, 18, 20, 22

infection (in-FEK-shun) — an invasion by disease-causing microscopic germs or tiny animals (such as eelworms) 18

maize (MAYZ) — in Canada and the United States, maize is commonly known as corn, but elsewhere "corn" often refers to cereal crops, such as wheat, barley, and rye 18

microscope (MY-kroh-skope) — an instrument used to magnify very small things, even things too small to be seen with the naked eye or an ordinary magnifying glass 4, 6

microscopic (my-kroh-SKOP-ik) — so small that a microscope is needed to see it 4

parasites (PA-ruh-sites) — plants or animals that live off other plants or animals 6

species (SPEE-shees) — a type of plant or animal 18, 20

tentacles (TEN-tuh-kulz) — fingerlike parts of a plant or animal 22

INDEX